Most Memorable
Court Cases

Charles Boocock • Jennifer Yu

Series Editor
Jeffrey D. Wilhelm

Much thought, debate, and research went into choosing and ranking the 10 items in each book in this series. We realize that everyone has his or her own opinion of what is most significant, revolutionary, amazing, deadly, and so on. As you read, you may agree with our choices, or you may be surprised — and that's the way it should be!

Franklin Watts®

an imprint of

SCHOLASTIC

www.scholastic.com/librarypublishing

A Rubicon book published in association with Scholastic Inc.

Rubicon © 2008 Rubicon Publishing Inc.
www.rubiconpublishing.com

Associate Publishers: Kim Koh, Miriam Bardswich
Project Editor: Amy Land
Creative Director: Jennifer Drew
Project Manager/Designer: Jeanette MacLean
Graphic Designers: Kristy Black, Jen Harvey

The publisher gratefully acknowledges the following for permission to reprint copyrighted material in this book.

Every reasonable effort has been made to trace the owners of copyrighted material and to make due acknowledgment. Any errors or omissions drawn to our attention will be gladly rectified in future editions.

"Copyright Myths" (excerpt) from "10 Big Myths About Copyright Explained" by Brad Templeton. Reprinted with permission.

Cover image: Linda Brown (left) with her parents Leola and Oliver and little sister Terry Lynn stand in front of their house, Topeka, Kansas, 1954. (Photo by Carl Iwasaki/Time Life Pictures/Getty Images)

Library and Archives Canada Cataloguing in Publication

Boocock, Charles
    The 10 most memorable court cases / Charles Boocock & Jennifer Yu.

ISBN: 978-1-55448-548-2

    1. Readers (Elementary). 2. Readers—Law—Cases.
I. Yu, Jennifer II. Title. III. Title: Ten most memorable court cases.

PE1117.B657 2007   428.6   C2007-906948-7

1 2 3 4 5 6 7 8 9 10   10   17 16 15 14 13 12 11 10 09 08

Printed in Singapore

Contents

Introduction: Lay Down the Law 4

Flood v. Kuhn 6
One professional baseball player challenged Major League Baseball and changed the rights of pro athletes forever.

Palsgraf v. Long Island Railroad Co. 10
Helen Palsgraf suffered injuries at a train station. Find out what happened when she sued the railroad company.

Liebeck v. McDonald's Restaurants 14
Spilled coffee led to one of the most publicized cases of the 1990s.

Tennessee Valley Authority v. Hill 18
A small fish, the federal government, and environmentalists brought about a landmark decision.

Sony Corp. v. Universal City Studios, Inc. 22
A new kind of technology can sometimes lead to legal trouble.

Commonwealth v. Sacco & Vanzetti 26
This trial was short and swift, but it caused a worldwide public outcry.

United States v. Nixon 30
A major political scandal resulted in one of the most famous legal decisions in U.S. history.

New York Times v. Sullivan 34
Freedom of the press was defended in this important case.

Gideon v. Wainwright 38
The court refused to give Clarence Gideon a lawyer. Read on to see whether this made his trial unfair.

Brown v. Board of Education of Topeka ... 42
This landmark case went beyond education — it changed the lives of Americans.

We Thought 46

What Do You Think? 47

Index 48

LAY DOWN THE LAW

Have you ever been in a courthouse? Or watched the television series *Law & Order*? The atmosphere is tense as the court decides the fate of the accused. The judges in their black robes, peering down from behind imposing desks, can make even hardened criminals shake. The bailiffs keep everyone quiet and the court under control; the lawyers on both sides present evidence and argue their case; and the jury makes the ultimate decision — guilty or innocent?

Judges don't just send criminals to prison. They help people settle their disputes peacefully. They ensure that everyone, from ordinary folks to the president, follows the law. Sometimes judges, especially justices of the United States Supreme Court, even help to define the law.

In the pages that follow, you'll find what we consider the 10 most memorable court cases in U.S. history. All these cases involved landmark decisions that have brought about significant changes in American society. In choosing and ranking these cases, we considered the following criteria: How much of an impact did the decision have on the legal system? On society? To what extent does the decision continue to influence rulings made in new cases? How much interest did the case stir up in the media? Was it hotly debated by the press? Among the public? Were there any particularly memorable incidents or facts surrounding the case?

As you read, consider how the various courts of the United States hear cases and decide on their rulings. Think like a judge and ask yourself:

---

landmark: *historic; significant*

WHICH OF THESE COURT CASES IS THE MOST MEMORABLE?

10 FLOOD V. KUHN

Curt Flood, in the midst of a legal battle with Major League Baseball, is shown here being interviewed by famed sportscaster Howard Cosell.

NEWSFLASH: BASEBALL STAR CHALLENGES PROFESSIONAL BASEBALL

MOMENT OF TRUTH: The United States Supreme Court issued its decision on June 19, 1972.

WHAT'S MEMORABLE: Curt Flood lost his baseball career but paved the way for free agency in professional baseball.

Today, professional baseball has a very busy off-season. When the games finish in October, hundreds of players' contracts expire, and the players are free to sign with any team. Teams fight to keep their best players and to sign new ones.

But it wasn't always this way. For decades, all baseball contracts included something called the reserve clause. When a player signed his first contract, that clause tied him to his team for the rest of his career. If his contract expired and he wanted to keep playing, the player had to make a new deal with his team. No other team could sign him unless his team traded him or released him from his contract.

In 1969, Curt Flood, a center fielder, was one of baseball's top players. He had been an All-Star three times and won seven straight Gold Gloves. He was co-captain of the St. Louis Cardinals and had led the team to two World Series championships.

After the season, St. Louis did not renew its contract with Flood. Instead, St. Louis traded Flood to the Philadelphia Phillies. Flood was shocked — so shocked that he refused to report to his new team. He sued Major League Baseball commissioner, Bowie K. Kuhn, arguing that the reserve clause illegally stopped him from signing with whichever team he wanted. The case became known as *Flood v. Kuhn*. It drew a lot of publicity, but did Flood win his case?

Gold Gloves: *award given to the best defensive player for each of the nine fielding positions in both the National and American Leagues*

FLOOD V. KUHN

THE ISSUE

Was the reserve clause, used in all baseball contracts, legal? Flood argued that the system was similar to slavery, because players couldn't choose where to work. The clause also kept players' salaries low, because if a player didn't like his team's contract offer, he couldn't play anywhere else. Flood argued that players should be free to work for the team that offered the highest salary.

 Do you think it was fair to compare the reserve clause system to slavery? Why or why not?

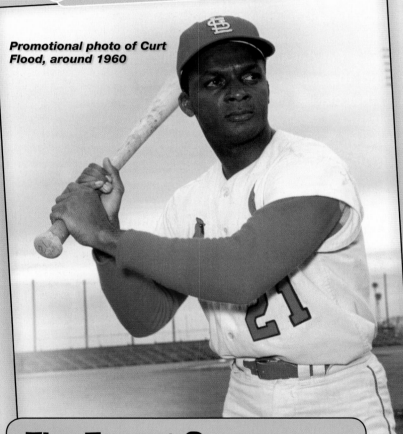

Promotional photo of Curt Flood, around 1960

The Expert Says...

" He [Curt Flood] really changed the way the game is paid, not played. "

— Gary Sales, a sports sociologist from Indiana University

THE DECISION

The Supreme Court had previously ruled that baseball's reserve clause was legal. The Court didn't want to contradict itself or disrupt an existing system that was based on the reserve clause. The Court, therefore, ruled against Flood on the grounds that the reserve clause had been considered legal since 1922. The justices of the Supreme Court were uneasy with their ruling, but they felt bound by precedent.

 Courts don't like to overrule their earlier decisions. Why do you think this is?

THE IMPACT

It took a lot of courage for Flood to challenge the reserve clause. In the end it cost him his career. However, it was not all in vain. Even though Flood lost the case, he had opened the door for future baseball players by making the public aware of the reserve clause and how unfair it was. In 1975, two players, Andy Messersmith and Dale McNally, won a similar case against Major League Baseball — leading to the free agency system. Players whose contracts expired were now free to switch teams. Some went on to become superstars with huge salaries, because teams had to compete for top players by offering the most attractive contracts.

precedent: *legal decision that serves as a guide for later cases*

Quick Fact

When Flood took his case to the courts, the average salary in Major League Baseball was about $25,000. The minimum salary had just reached $10,000 — after being stuck at $6,000 for two decades — and most players spent their entire career playing for the same team.

10   9   8   7   6

Flood lost his case, but he won big time for the professional baseball players who came after him. Since the arrival of free agency, their salaries have skyrocketed, as shown in the following chart.

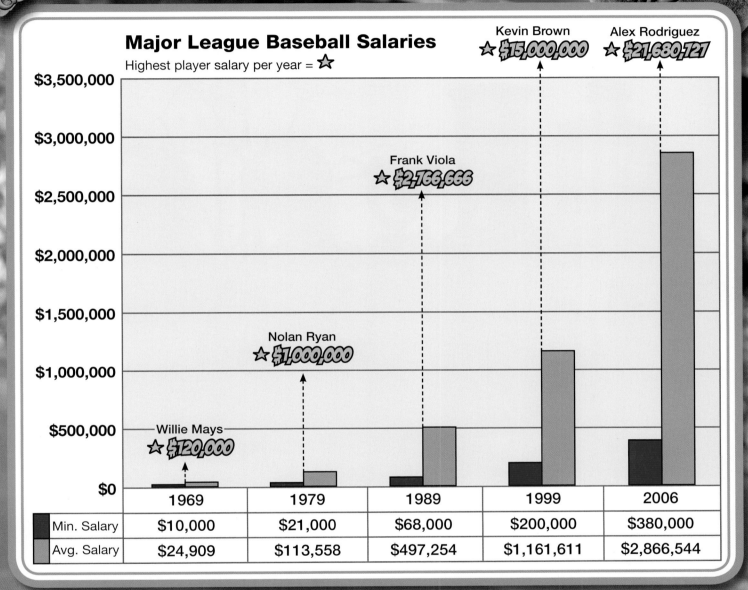

Major League Baseball Salaries

Highest player salary per year = ☆

Willie Mays ☆ $120,000
Nolan Ryan ☆ $1,000,000
Frank Viola ☆ $2,766,666
Kevin Brown ☆ $15,000,000
Alex Rodriguez ☆ $21,680,727

	1969	1979	1989	1999	2006
Min. Salary	$10,000	$21,000	$68,000	$200,000	$380,000
Avg. Salary	$24,909	$113,558	$497,254	$1,161,611	$2,866,544

? Free agency increases competition among teams for good players. As a result, top players are making big, fat salaries. Do you think this is good for the game? Why or why not?

Quick Fact

Flood refused to report to Philadelphia and sat out the entire 1970 season. That November, Flood was traded to the Washington Senators. But his skills were rusty after a year off, and he ended his career in 1971.

Take Note

Flood v. Kuhn swings into the #10 spot. This case shows what one person of passion and courage can achieve. Flood sacrificed his career to fight for the rights of baseball players. Even though the Supreme Court ruled against him, his well-publicized case won public support and in the end led to important changes in baseball, the most important of which was the free agency system.

• Flood made a huge personal sacrifice in his fight for the rights of baseball players. Which cause would you make personal sacrifices to fight for and why?

5   4   3   2   1

The Long Island Railroad Company made headlines in the 1920s when a passenger sued for injury compensation

EARLY LONG ISLAND RAILROAD (LIRR) TRAIN—© BETTMANN/CORBIS

ISLAND RAILROAD CO.

NEWSFLASH: HOUSEKEEPER INJURED ON LONG ISLAND RAILROAD PLATFORM

MOMENT OF TRUTH: The New York Court of Appeals made its decision on May 29, 1928.

WHAT'S MEMORABLE: This was a landmark ruling on foreseeability — whether a person can predict the consequences of an action. It raises the question of whether a person should be held responsible for causing an unpredictable harm.

On August 24, 1924, Helen Palsgraf and her two daughters were standing on a Long Island Railroad platform waiting for a train. Suddenly, at the far end of the station, two men raced onto the platform and jumped onto the car of a train that was already leaving. One of them barely made it, and appeared to be falling off. Two railroad employees reached out to help. In the confusion, a package the passenger was holding fell to the platform. The package contained fireworks, which exploded loudly. The blast could be heard several blocks away. It toppled a large scale standing near Helen Palsgraf. The scale struck her in the arm, hip, and thigh.

As a result of the injuries, Palsgraf could walk only with great difficulty. She also suffered from shock-related symptoms, including stuttering. Palsgraf was unable to continue her job as a housekeeper. She sued the Long Island Railroad, claiming her injuries resulted from the negligence of its employee.

Would Helen Palsgraf win the lawsuit? Was the employee at fault? *Palsgraf v. Long Island Railroad Company* became one of the most debated cases of all time. What was the ruling of the court? Read on to find out.

---

negligence: *defined by the courts as a failure to act with reasonable care toward others*
lawsuit: *when an individual seeks to settle a dispute in court (also known as a suit)*

PALSGRAF V. LONG ISLAND RAILROAD CO.

Quick Fact

In most states, the Supreme Court is the highest court of appeal. But in New York the Supreme Court is actually a trial court, where cases are first filed. The Supreme Court's decisions can be challenged at the New York Court of Appeals, which is New York State's highest court.

THE ISSUE

The railroad employees were simply trying to help a passenger get on board the train. They didn't know that the passenger's parcel contained fireworks, so Helen Palsgraf's injury was accidental and unexpected. Should the railroad company be liable for this?

THE DECISION

On May 26, 1927, the Supreme Court of the State of New York awarded Helen Palsgraf $6,000 in damages, based on a trial jury's verdict. The railroad appealed the decision. One year later, Chief Judge Benjamin Cardozo of the New York Court of Appeals ruled that the railroad was not responsible. He explained that the actions of the railroad employee had not been negligent and that the contents of the package were unknown. The package was wrapped in newspaper, and there was nothing in the appearance of the package to suggest that it contained explosives. The judge decided if the railroad worker had no idea that by helping one passenger he could end up hurting another — if he couldn't "foresee" the accident — then he shouldn't be punished. Helen Palsgraf got nothing.

---

liable: *legally responsible for, often involving payment for damage or injury caused*

appealed: *challenged the decision in a higher court*

? Do you think the ruling would be different if the *Palsgraf* incident occurred today? Why?

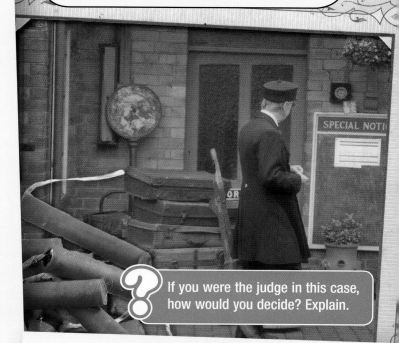

? If you were the judge in this case, how would you decide? Explain.

THE IMPACT

In *Palsgraf*, the court defined the limits of responsibility that individuals have toward one another. By only allowing people with "foreseeable" injuries to sue for compensation, it established the foundation for today's personal injury law. It is one of the most debated tort cases of all time. Almost no student graduates from law school without studying it!

---

tort: *wrongful act that results in injuries to another person, and for which the injured person can sue for compensation*

The Expert Says...

"This [*Palsgraf v. Long Island Railroad Co.*] became one of the most debated tort cases of all time, the foundation of much negligence law."

— Paul E. Pfeifer, Ohio Supreme Court justice

The Palsgraf Curse

DESCENDANTS OF HELEN PALSGRAF BELIEVE HER CASE STARTED A CURSE ON THE FAMILY. READ ABOUT THEIR ACCIDENTS IN THE FOLLOWING ANECDOTES.

1. WILLIAM PALSGRAF JR., HELEN'S GRANDSON

In 1965, he rented a ladder to put an antenna on the roof of his house. The ladder collapsed and he fell three floors onto his driveway. He broke his arm and wrist. He claimed the ladder was defective and sued the manufacturer. The suit never made it to court because the ladder was stolen from the courtroom!

2. BARBARA PALSGRAF, THE WIFE OF WILLIAM PALSGRAF JR.

She was trying to move a ping-pong table at the school where she was a teacher. The table collapsed and injured her thumb. After three operations, the thumb was amputated. Ms. Barbara Palsgraf sued the school but the proceedings took so long that she settled for what she described as "peanuts."

3. WILLIAM PALSGRAF III, SON OF BARBARA AND WILLIAM PALSGRAF JR.

In 1970, while in high school, William Palsgraf III was jogging when he stumbled over a broken curb and broke his ankle. The family thought about suing, but attorneys discouraged them from doing so.

Take Note

The *Palsgraf v. Long Island Railroad Co.* case takes the #9 spot. This landmark 1928 ruling has guided later decisions involving tort law, negligence, and compensation awards for injuries. Even today, when negligence suits arise, lawyers on both sides will revisit *Palsgraf*.

• Based on all the aspects of this case, do you agree it should be required reading for law students? Give your reasons.

5   4   3   2   1

Stella Liebeck has her day in court.

NALD'S RESTAURANTS

NEWSFLASH: CORPORATE GIANT SUED FOR SERVING HOT COFFEE

MOMENT OF TRUTH: On August 18, 1994, the jury in Albuquerque, New Mexico, gave its verdict on Stella Liebeck's suit against McDonald's Restaurants.

WHAT'S MEMORABLE: The court judgment made headlines and gave rise to the phrase "Stella Award."

The tale of the spilled coffee case began on February 27, 1992. Stella Liebeck was sitting in the passenger seat of a car driven by her grandson. After ordering a cup of coffee at a McDonald's drive-through, her grandson parked the car so that Liebeck could add cream and sugar. She placed the cup between her knees, but failed to remove the lid properly. Instead, she spilled the entire cup of coffee. She suffered third-degree burns.

Liebeck was hospitalized for eight days, and had to undergo painful skin grafting. It took two years for her to fully recover. Liebeck sought to settle for $20,000 to cover medical costs, but McDonald's refused. Liebeck decided to sue.

The jury in New Mexico found Liebeck to be partly responsible but concluded that McDonald's was largely to blame. In 1994, the court awarded Stella Liebeck a whopping $2.7 million.

Liebeck's unfortunate coffee spill resulted in the infamous "McDonald's Coffee Case."

---

third-degree burns: *severe burns that destroy both the outer layer of skin (epidermis) and the layer underneath (dermis)*
skin grafting: *surgery in which wounded skin is replaced with healthy skin removed from another part of the patient's body*
settle: *end a legal dispute by mutual agreement, without going to court*

LIEBECK V. McDONALD'S RESTAURANTS

THE ISSUE

The question was whether McDonald's disregarded customer safety by serving coffee at 180 to 190°F. Was its coffee unreasonably dangerous? McDonald's lawyers argued that the National Coffee Association recommended serving coffee at that temperature for best flavor. They also presented statistics showing that over a 10-year period, McDonald's had served 24 million cups of coffee, causing only 700 injuries.

THE DECISION

The statistics presented by the defense worked against McDonald's. They showed that the company knew its coffee was hot enough to cause injury. The judge called McDonald's conduct "reckless, callous, and willful." The jury's initial award to Liebeck was $200,000 in aggravated damages. This amount was later reduced to $160,000 because the jury held Liebeck partly responsible for the incident. However, they also awarded Liebeck $2.7 million in punitive damages. This was much more than the $20,000 she had originally asked for!

---

aggravated damages: *intended to compensate for injuries*

punitive damages: *intended to punish the defendant for wrongdoing, and no proof of injury is required*

The Expert Says...

" In my opinion, the decision makes me feel that life in the United States is constantly being tested for the safety of its citizens. Furthermore, having the ability for recourse against large corporations makes the society a much safer place. "

— Albuquerque civil court clerk

---

recourse: *right to seek payment or take action*

? Why do you think the media became so fascinated with *Liebeck v. McDonald's*?

Quick Fact

Following the *Liebeck* decision, the term "Stella Award" has often been used to refer to any lawsuit that sounds outrageous.

THE IMPACT

The trial judge reduced the punitive damages award to $480,000. In the end, the two parties settled for an undisclosed amount. This case was highly publicized by the media. After the huge settlement, many people were pleased that a big corporation was made to pay for negligence and misconduct. To some the case was an example of how the law can be used to hold a corporation accountable to its customers and to the public. Others were concerned that the publicity of the case would cause a rise in frivolous claims and abuses of tort law.

---

undisclosed: *not revealed to the public*
frivolous: *silly and trivial*

? Why do you think McDonald's and Liebeck decided on the amount of compensation privately? Present your views from the standpoint of both parties.

Quick Fact

This case was spoofed in an episode of the popular TV show, *Seinfeld*.

? Read the quote from this expert carefully to understand what is being said. Explain why you agree or disagree with the statement.

THE JURY'S DECISION

There have been many jokes made by individuals or groups about the *Liebeck* case. What do you think? Was it a frivolous lawsuit? Was Stella Liebeck a greedy person? Was McDonald's negligent to serve such hot coffee to its customers? Was the compensation fair or outrageous? This list sheds more light on the case.

1. Between 1982 and 1992, more than 700 incidents of injuries from McDonald's coffee had been reported to the company. Some were minor burns, and others were third-degree burns. Children were among those who suffered injuries.

2. Before the *Liebeck* lawsuit, McDonald's served coffee at 190°F. It takes less than three seconds to produce a third-degree burn at this temperature. Coffee is usually served at between 135 and 140°F.

3. McDonald's served such hot coffee in its drive-through windows because it thought people would take the coffee home, and McDonald's wanted the coffee to stay hot. However, the company's own research showed that customers actually consumed their coffee in the car.

4. According to a McDonald's executive, the company knew that its coffee could cause serious burns at that temperature. But they thought the number of complaints was insignificant, considering they sold millions of cups of coffee every year.

5. Since the Liebeck incident, coffee at the Albuquerque McDonald's is now served at 158°F.

? Do you think the jury would have decided differently if Stella Liebeck had scalded herself with coffee that she purchased from a small neighborhood store? Explain.

Take Note

Liebeck v. McDonald's Restaurants takes the #8 spot. The case serves as a warning that businesses will be held responsible for practices that disregard public safety. Thanks to the case, businesses now display signs and warnings to alert everyone to the slightest danger or risk.
• In what ways are the cases of *Liebeck* and *Palsgraf* similar or different?

5   4   3   2   1

7 TENNESSEE VALLEY

Damming the Little Tennessee River created the Tellico Reservoir in Tennessee.

AUTHORITY V. HILL

NEWSFLASH: LITTLE FISH HALTS DAM PROJECT

MOMENT OF TRUTH: The United States Supreme Court pulled the plug on the dam on June 15, 1978.

WHAT'S MEMORABLE: Discovery of a small fish — an endangered species — halted construction of a large dam being built by the Tennessee Valley Authority.

In October 1974, Hank Hill was a law student at the University of Tennessee. He had to write a 10-page essay about environmental law, but he couldn't find a topic! Then he learned that an endangered fish species had been discovered in the Little Tennessee River. It was a small fish called the snail darter. Hill had found his topic. He wrote about the fish, the new Endangered Species Act (ESA), and the Tellico Dam that was being built by the Tennessee Valley Authority (TVA).

For many years, local dairy farmers had tried to stop the building of the dam because it would create a large lake flooding their farmlands. The native Cherokee Nation also opposed the project because their ancestral burial sites would be submerged. These efforts had been unsuccessful, but Hill's essay described how a petition to stop the dam might be made under the ESA.

In its decision, the Supreme Court upheld the terms of the ESA. The law banned the federal government from funding projects that would harm an endangered species and the Court enforced that ban. It was a groundbreaking judgment that placed the ESA at the forefront of today's environmental law.

---

ancestral: *left behind by earlier generations*
petition: *written formal request seeking a specific court action*
groundbreaking: *relating to something not done before*

TENNESSEE VALLEY AUTHORITY V. HILL

The snail darter is a variety of fish that feeds on snails; it is found in the waters of eastern Tennessee.

THE ISSUE

The Tellico Dam was being built by the Tennessee Valley Authority, a power company wholly owned by the federal government. By damming the river, the project threatened to kill off the snail darter, an endangered fish that lived on snails found in the river's shallow flowing water. Millions of dollars had been spent, and the dam was near completion. So could the project be stopped?

Quick Fact

Tellico Dam is one of approximately 80,000 dams in the United States. It doesn't generate electricity. Instead, it makes it easier for boats to navigate the Little Tennessee River and allows another dam on a nearby river to produce more electricity. It also helps control flooding.

The Tellico Dam cost approximately $141 million to build.

Dams are costly to build and maintain, and environmentalists are often opposed to their construction. What are the pros and cons of dam projects?

THE DECISION

The trial court in Tennessee had ruled in favor of the TVA for several reasons: construction of the Tellico Dam had been approved by the United States Congress in 1967, seven years before the ESA; the dam was near completion; and 95 percent of the budget had already been spent. But the Supreme Court rejected the trial court's decision. Tellico Dam threatened to destroy an endangered species' habitat. Under the ESA, therefore, Congress was not allowed to fund it, and the project had to be halted.

THE IMPACT

TVA v. Hill brought national attention to the environmental movement. It made people think about how best to balance nature and development. It made corporations think hard before launching projects that could threaten the environment. It also caused Congress to rewrite the ESA to allow for exceptions. The Tellico Dam eventually did open, thanks to one of these exceptions. But the fish survived. Snail darters were later discovered in five other local rivers.

Snail darters were later found in five other rivers. Does this mean the Supreme Court's 1978 ruling was incorrect? Explain.

The Expert Says...

"The real story was never the snail darter. It was the river. It was about resisting the willy-nilly remaking of the natural environment at the behest of industry.

— Andrew Leonard, senior writer at salon.com

behest: *strongly worded request or demand*

10   9   8   **7**   6

WINNER AND LOSER

Tennessee Valley Authority v. Hill looked like a lopsided fight. It was a case of a small fish battling a giant multimillion-dollar project approved and funded by the federal government. For more details, read this comparison chart.

	SNAIL DARTER	TELLICO DAM
Appearance	Usually less than an inch long, but the biggest snail darters can reach three inches in length.	The dam stands 129 feet high. It spans 3,238 feet across the Little Tennessee River.
How Many?	The construction of nearby dams had caused a massive decline in the snail darter population. Researchers feared that those near the dam were the last of the species. Further research discovered more snail darters living nearby. With careful conservation and the transplanting of snail darters to other rivers, there are now nine separate populations, each numbering in the hundreds.	Tellico was only one dam, and it was one of the smaller dams built by TVA. But the entire TVA system included more than 60 dams, including five on the Little Tennessee River.
Representatives	Zygmunt Plater, Hank Hill's environmental law professor at the University of Tennessee, argued for the fish.	United States Attorney General Griffin Bell led the TVA's defense of the dam.
Records	Two Wins — One Loss. The snail darter lost in the District Court, which refused to halt construction at Tellico. But the United States Court of Appeals and the Supreme Court both reversed the lower court.	One Win — Two Losses. The dam's initial victory was reversed by the United States Court of Appeals, which voted to stop the project. So did the Supreme Court.

Fontana Dam is a Tennessee Valley Authority (TVA) dam on the Little Tennessee River.

Take Note

Tennessee Valley Authority v. Hill takes the #7 spot. It is a powerful example of citizens using the courts to influence government policy. By quickly recognizing the snail darter's significance, Hill managed to stop the Tellico Dam project. More importantly, this case resulted in a landmark decision that brought the ESA into the spotlight.

• Research the ESA and provide answers for these questions: How does an endangered species get listed? How many species are currently protected by the ESA? How are listed species protected?

2   1

Although the movie studios took Sony to court, the entertainment industry later benefited from selling video recordings of movies, music, and other productions.

AL CITY STUDIOS, INC.

NEWSFLASH: SONY TAKEN TO COURT FOR ITS VIDEOTAPE RECORDER

MOMENT OF TRUTH: On January 17, 1984, the United States Supreme Court ruled on Universal Studios' claim that Sony's videotape recorder helped and encouraged users to violate copyright.

WHAT'S MEMORABLE: This was the first case to challenge technologies designed to copy copyrighted works.

In 1975, Sony Corporation of Japan launched the Betamax, an early version of the videocassette recorder (VCR). This home video technology could record and play back TV programs and movies. This was a time when much of today's digital technology did not exist. There were none of the CD players, home video games, cell phones, digital cameras, or portable media players, that we now take for granted.

In early 1976, Sony introduced Betamax in the United States. Because the machines let viewers tape television shows for later viewing, the movie studios felt threatened. They feared that this new product would cut audiences for their programming and, as a result, reduce their income. So they filed a lawsuit against Sony. They asked the court to ban VCR sales, claiming that helping consumers to copy TV shows was an infringement of their copyright.

Sony Corp. v. Universal City Studios, Inc., commonly referred to as the Betamax Case, went to trial on January 30, 1979. The court battles lasted over four years and the case went all the way to the Supreme Court of the United States.

---

infringement: *violation*
copyright: *exclusive rights held by a work's creator to sell, publish, copy, or distribute that work*

SONY CORP. V. UNIVERSAL CITY STUDIOS, INC.

THE ISSUE

The studios argued that VCRs allowed, and even encouraged, buyers to violate copyright laws by making unauthorized copies of copyrighted programs. Sony argued that the VCR could be used for general recording, and not solely for taping of copyrighted broadcasts. It also stated that consumers had the absolute right to record programs at home for private use, and that the company could not be legally responsible for their actions.

THE DECISION

Different courts reached very different decisions about this new technology. In 1979, after a five-week trial, the district court ruled in Sony's favor, finding that the Copyright Act did not ban personal recordings made for watching at home. The studios challenged that decision in the court of appeals. In 1981, that court overruled the trial court, finding that VCR use did harm copyright holders. Now Sony appealed. Three years later, the Supreme Court made the final decision in Sony's favor. That Court stated that recording for home viewing at a later time constituted a "fair use" of the copyright material.

---

unauthorized: *without permission*
fair use: *an exception to copyright infringement, allowing unauthorized use of copyrighted work if that use won't harm the copyright holder*

Which of the rulings do you agree with? Why?

Quick Fact

In 1975, the Betamax videotape stored one hour of video. A year later, a competing company released the VHS (video home system) tape, which could hold two hours of video. Later VHS tapes could store four or more hours of video, and VHS soon took control of the market.

THE IMPACT

This landmark case on the sale and use of videotape recording technology has had a huge impact. By slightly lowering copyright protection, it allowed Sony to continue selling VCRs, and paved the way for future recording technologies. The decision has protected technology innovators over the years from lawsuits filed by music and movie giants. Companies such as Internet service providers, Internet search engines, and software developers all sell products that can help consumers access copyrighted material without paying for it. When sued for copyright infringement, these companies have relied on the Betamax Case to defend their products.

The Expert Says...

" [The court] declared that Sony was not violating copyright laws by selling [VCRs], even though some people might use them to infringe copyrights. In other words, you don't go after the crowbar makers just because there are burglars out there. "

— Fred von Lohmann, senior intellectual property attorney, Electronic Frontier Foundation

What do you think Fred von Lohmann meant in the last sentence? You might wish to use a different example in your explanation.

COPYRIGHT MYTHS

Copyright infringement is a major issue, and yet most people are not clear about the law. How much do you know? Read these fact cards to find out.

Extracted from "10 Big Myths About Copyright Explained" by Brad Templeton

If it doesn't have a copyright notice, it's not copyrighted.

Not true today. Almost everything created in the United States after April 1, 1989, is copyrighted and protected whether it has a notice or not. For works created before that date, the rules are more complicated. The default you should assume for other people's works is that they are copyrighted and may not be copied unless you know otherwise.

default: *conclusion that occurs automatically because no alternatives exist*

If it is posted to Usenet it's in the public domain [meaning that anyone can use it because it's not protected by copyright].

False. Nothing modern and creative is in the public domain anymore unless the owner explicitly puts it in the public domain, with a note saying "I grant this to the public domain."

Usenet: *online bulletin board where people post and read articles*

 Do you think it is wrong to download music and movies for personal use? Why or why not?

If I don't charge for it, it's not a violation.

False. Whether you charge can affect the damages awarded in court, but that's the main difference under the law. It's still a violation if you give it away — and there can still be serious damages if you hurt the commercial value of the property. If the work has no commercial value, the violation is mostly technical and is unlikely to result in legal action.

If I make up my own stories, but base them on another work, my new work belongs to me.

False. U.S. copyright law is quite explicit that the making of works based on or derived from another copyrighted work is the exclusive province of the owner of the original work. ... If you write a story using settings or characters from somebody else's work, you need that author's permission.

Take Note

Sony Corp. v. Universal City Studios, Inc. claims the #6 spot. This case paved the way for the development of new recording technologies. It is still used as a reference to help information technology companies defend against claims of copyright infringement.

• Find out more about the meaning of "fair use" as it relates to copyright. How does it apply to the downloading of material from the Internet?

5   4   3   2   1

Nicola Sacco (1891–1927) and Bartolomeo Vanzetti (1888–1927) in jail before their execution in 1927.

SACCO & VANZETTI

NEWSFLASH: WORLDWIDE ANGER OVER SACCO & VANZETTI VERDICT

MOMENT OF TRUTH: Sacco and Vanzetti were found guilty of murder on July 14, 1921.

WHAT'S MEMORABLE: The case became one of the most infamous criminal trials in U.S. history. It showed that significant reforms were needed to fix the U.S. justice system.

On the afternoon of April 15, 1920, a Boston shoe factory's paymaster and his guard were shot and killed in broad daylight. Their cargo, nearly $16,000 in payroll, was snatched up by the killers, who sped off in a getaway car. Witnesses described the two killers as looking like Italians. Three weeks later, Nicola Sacco and Bartolomeo Vanzetti were arrested and charged with the double murder. The trial lasted only six weeks. Both were found guilty and sentenced to death.

Sacco and Vanzetti were poor Italian immigrants. They were members of an Italian political group known for its violence. The group had carried out several bombings and assassination attempts. From the time of their arrest, things didn't go well for the two men. They were both carrying guns when arrested. Many saw this, and the fact that both had lied about the guns, as proof of their guilt. Although Sacco and Vanzetti had strong alibis, these were undermined by conflicting evidence and testimony at their trial. Worse, the presiding judge, Webster Thayer, and some jury members had publicly expressed ethnic bias against the two men. When another person confessed to the murder before the guilty verdict was announced it looked like Sacco and Vanzetti might walk away free. But both were still found guilty. Despite public outcry and many appeals, the two men were executed on August 23, 1927.

---

paymaster: *person hired by a company to pay wages and salaries*
alibis: *explanations that the accused were somewhere else at the time of the crime*
presiding: *one who directs or regulates proceedings; judge hearing a case*

COMMONWEALTH V. SACCO & VANZETTI

Nicola Sacco and Bartolomeo Vanzetti handcuffed together at the Dedham courthouse.

THE ISSUE

Did the two men get a fair trial? Did the court focus on evidence relating to the double murder, or were the two men punished for their involvement with a criminal Italian group? Evidence suggested the defendants had been elsewhere at the time of the murders and that their guns hadn't been used. The prosecution, however, focused on their beliefs and ethnicity. In addition, the presiding judge, Webster Thayer, had previously tried Vanzetti for another crime, and had specifically asked to try Sacco and Vanzetti for the double murder. He was overheard saying he would "get them good and proper."

THE DECISION

Sacco and Vanzetti were quickly convicted of murder and sentenced to death. For a trial with such conflicting and contradictory evidence, the jury took only a few hours to return a unanimous guilty verdict for both men.

---

prosecution: *attorney who represents the government in criminal trial*
unanimous: *with everyone in agreement*

? Do you think racial and ethnic biases can influence the outcome of a trial today? Explain.

THE IMPACT

The case sparked public outcry and massive protests around the world. It led to a new law, which gave the Massachusetts Supreme Judicial Court the power to order a new trial if the verdict contradicted the evidence presented or if new evidence surfaced. After the trial, it was decided that only evidence that is directly related to the crime can be presented to the jury. The Sacco and Vanzetti trial would go on to influence the United States Supreme Court to issue several important decisions. Under Chief Justice Earl Warren, the Supreme Court extended due process protection and the right to a fair trial.

---

due process: *legal principle that guarantees a person's full legal rights when government action could deprive that person of life, liberty, or property*

SAVE SACCO & VANZ
PROTEST DEMONSTRATION AGAINST DEATH S
TRAFALGAR SQUARE, SUNDAY NE
COME IN YOUR THOUSANDS

Protest to save Sacco and Vanzetti in London, England, in 1921.

Quick Fact

Massachusetts Governor Michael Dukakis proclaimed August 23, 1977, "Nicola Sacco and Bartolomeo Vanzetti Memorial Day" to mark the 50th anniversary of their death.

The Expert Says...

"Whatever the truth of their guilt or innocence, no other crime story of our century has spawned so many poems, plays, novels, and passionate works of history. ... No other case has defined an era of American history ... [better] than the trial and fate of these two immigrant Italians."

— Russell Aiuto, Director of Research and Development, National Science Teachers Association

spawned: *gave rise to; inspired*

THEIR FINAL WORDS

Sacco and Vanzetti fought the guilty verdict until the end. They wrote many letters to friends and family members while in prison. This is a shortened version of their final letter to thank those who fought along with them.

Dear Friends and Comrades of the Sacco-Vanzetti Defense Committee:

After tomorrow mid-night, we will be executed, save a new staying of the execution by either the United States Supreme Court or by Governor Alvan T. Fuller.

We have no hope. This morning, our brave defender and friend Michael Angelo Musmanno was here from his return from Washington, and told us he would come back this afternoon if he would have time for it. But now it is 5:30 P.M. and no one returned yet. ... In a word, we feel lost! Therefore, we decided to write this letter to you to express our gratitude and admiration for all what you have done in our defense during these seven years, four months, and 11 days of struggle.

That we lost and have to die does not diminish our appreciation and gratitude for your great solidarity with us and our families.

Be all as of one heart in this blackest hour of our tragedy. And have heart.

We embrace you all, and bid you all our extreme good-bye with our hearts filled with love and affection. Now and ever, long life to you all, long life to Liberty.

Yours in life and death,

BARTOLOMEO VANZETTI
NICOLA SACCO

save: *without; but for*

 If Sacco and Vanzetti had an unfair trial, what should have been done? Should a new trial have been held? Should they have been set free? Explain.

Quick Fact

After the Sacco-Vanzetti case, Chief Justice Thayer became extremely unpopular. His home was bombed in an assassination attempt and he had to live under 24-hour security protection.

Take Note

Commonwealth v. Sacco & Vanzetti secures the #5 spot on our list. This simple murder trial raised important issues of legal fairness and led to significant changes in the way trials are conducted. This case continues to be examined and revisited by lawmakers, historians, and legal reformers.
• Do you think that Sacco and Vanzetti had a fair trial? Make a list of your reasons.

5
4
3
2
1

On August 9, 1974, President Richard Nixon resigned from the presidency after the Watergate scandal. Vice President Gerald Ford was sworn in as the 38th president.

V. NIXON

NEWSFLASH: WATERGATE INVESTIGATION LEADS TO WHITE HOUSE

MOMENT OF TRUTH: On July 24, 1974, the Supreme Court issued its decision on whether President Richard Nixon must hand over the Watergate tapes.

WHAT'S MEMORABLE: Watergate was a major political scandal. It resulted in one of the most famous legal decisions in the United States.

The Watergate scandal started slowly. On June 17, 1972, five men were arrested while breaking into the Watergate Hotel in Washington, D.C. They carried tape recorders and were suspected of plotting to bug the Democratic Party's offices.

Soon, a bigger picture began to unfold. Carl Bernstein and Bob Woodward, two reporters covering the story, discovered that the burglars were employed by President Nixon's re-election committee. They uncovered other efforts by the committee to sabotage the president's political opponents. These activities were unethical, and sometimes illegal. They appeared to be organized and paid for by the White House. This was the start of what would become known as the Watergate affair.

The U.S. Senate appointed a special prosecutor to investigate. He was shocked to learn that President Nixon had secretly taped all his Oval Office conversations. Thinking that the tapes contained important evidence, the prosecutor ordered Nixon to hand over the tapes. But Nixon refused.

The White House faced heavy criticism. Finally, it turned over edited copies of some of the tapes, but not all of them. The district court judge threatened to hold the president in contempt of court. The United States Supreme Court agreed to hear the dispute. Can the Supreme Court judge the president? What do you think?

bug: *hide microphones or other electronic eavesdropping devices*
unethical: *morally wrong*
contempt of court: *legal punishment for disrespecting or disobeying a court order*

UNITED STATES V. NIXON

THE ISSUE

Did the president of the United States have to produce evidence in his possession if it was relevant to a criminal investigation? Nixon argued that, because he was president, he could simply choose not to cooperate with the investigation. The special prosecutor, Leon Jaworski, disagreed. He said the president's desire to keep his conversations private was less important than the need to establish the facts.

THE DECISION

The Court unanimously decided that not even the president of the United States had the right to withhold information relevant to a criminal investigation. It acknowledged that the president has special privilege on matters of diplomatic or national security, but that privilege is not absolute. The Court stressed that criminal justice requires all the relevant facts of a crime to be established, and noted that federal judges could inspect such information in private.

THE IMPACT

The Supreme Court stressed that no one is above the law, not even presidents. The Court was following a doctrine laid down in Magna Carta, a British document from 1215 stating that not even the king is above the law. The White House was ordered to produce all the tapes. Soon after hearing them, Congress began efforts to remove President Nixon from office. Nixon resigned on August 9, 1974, only three weeks after the Court's decision.

relevant: *related and important*
doctrine: *position or policy*

? On what grounds did the Supreme Court overrule the president's refusal to release the tapes? Do you agree with the Court's decision? Explain.

? Nixon argued that the tapes should be kept secret because his advisers might not speak candidly in future if their words could become public knowledge. If you knew your conversations could become public knowledge, would you be more or less likely to speak freely? Why?

Quick Fact

There are nine judges on the United States Supreme Court. But Justice William Rehnquist didn't participate in the *Nixon* ruling because he had previously worked for the president's administration.

Quick Fact

In 1973, the *Washington Post* won a Pulitzer Prize for its four-year investigation into the Watergate affair. The two reporters, Carl Bernstein and Bob Woodward, co-authored a best-selling book in 1976 about their investigation. It was entitled *All the President's Men,* and was later made into a movie.

The Expert Says...

" Only a few times in its history has the court grappled with such large assertions of governmental power. As in most of those encounters, the justices concluded that the judiciary must have the last word in an orderly constitutional system. ... "

— John P. MacKenzie, *Washington Post* staff writer

assertions: *claims*
judiciary: *system of courts of law and their judges*

The SMOKING GUN

Here is a partial transcript of a taped conversation between H. R. Haldeman and President Richard Nixon. It took place just six days after the Watergate break-in. Haldeman, the president's closest aide and chief of staff, expressed concern that the FBI could trace money found on the burglars to the White House. The transcript proved that Nixon was not only aware that his office had initiated the break-in but that he also helped plan the cover-up.

Haldeman: okay — that's fine. Now, on the investigation, you know, the Democratic break-in thing, we're back to the — in the, the problem area because the FBI is not under control, because Gray [L. Patrick Gray, Acting Director of the FBI at the time] doesn't exactly know how to control them, and they have, their investigation is now leading into some productive areas, because they've been able to trace the money, not through the money itself, but through the bank, you know, sources — the banker himself. And, and it goes in some directions we don't want it to go. Ah, also there have been some things, like an informant came in off the street to the FBI in Miami, who was a photographer or has a friend who is a photographer who developed some films through this guy, Barker [Bernard Leon Barker, a former member of the Cuban Secret Police, was one of the five burglars arrested in the Watergate break-in], and the films had pictures of Democratic National Committee letter head documents and things. ...

Haldeman: That the way to handle this now is for us to have Walters [Vernon Walters was then Deputy Director of the CIA] call Pat Gray and just say, "... this is ah, business here we don't want you to go any further on it." That's not an unusual development ...

Nixon: Um huh.

Haldeman: ... and, uh, that would take care of it. ...

Nixon: But they've traced the money to 'em.

Haldeman: Well they have, they've traced to a name, but they haven't gotten to the guy yet. ...

Haldeman: He's ah, he gave $25,000 in Minnesota and ah, the check went directly in to this, to this guy Barker.

? Because this is an actual conversation there are many pauses and grammatical errors. As you read, pick through those to find words or phrases that could be used as evidence against the president.

Quick Fact

In the history of the United States, only two presidents have been impeached — Andrew Jackson in 1868 and Bill Clinton in 1999. Both were found not guilty.

impeached: *formally accused of participating in illegal activities while in office*

Take Note

United States v. Nixon takes the #4 spot. When the Watergate scandal became public, Congress began investigating the White House. When the president would not cooperate, the courts had to settle the dispute. The court ruling brought down the president of the United States.

• In the search for truth, do you agree that everyone must reveal private information, even the president or leader of a country? Give your reasons.

5   **4**   3   2   1

Police Commissioner L.B. Sullivan (second from left) celebrates his $500,000 libel suit victory against the New York Times. From left are attorneys Roland Nachman, Sullivan, Calvin Whitesell, and Sam Rice Baker.

New York Time

Montgomery's Police Chie

MES V. SULLIVAN

NEWSFLASH: ALABAMA COURT ORDERS *NEW YORK TIMES* TO PAY MILLIONS OF DOLLARS FOR LIBEL

MOMENT OF TRUTH: The United States Supreme Court overruled the Alabama court's judgment on March 9, 1964.

WHAT'S MEMORABLE: The ruling ensured the future of the *New York Times* and freed the press to criticize public officials.

On March 29, 1960, the *New York Times* ran a full-page advertisement describing police brutality against African-American students in Montgomery, Alabama. L. B. Sullivan, the head of the police department in Montgomery, sued the *New York Times* for libel. He argued that even though his name was not mentioned, the advertisement was directed at him. The Supreme Court of Alabama awarded him $500,000 in damages.

This court decision put the *Times'* entire future in jeopardy. The newspaper's stories reporting on racial segregation and civil rights in the Southern states had been strongly criticized by white Southerners. Like other newspapers and news organizations, the *New York Times* faced many lawsuits and might go bankrupt if it were held accountable for libel.

The *New York Times* appealed the Alabama court's decision to the Supreme Court. It said that the libel judgment violated the Constitution's First Amendment, which guarantees freedom of the press. It argued that the decision would prevent the press from reporting the illegal actions of public officials who supported segregation. But what would be the decision of the Supreme Court?

libel: *written statement that unjustly damages the reputation of a person*
segregation: *separation of people with different skin colors as a form of discrimination*

V. Sul

warded $500,000 ...

NEW YORK TIMES V. SULLIVAN

The Supreme Court of the United States

THE ISSUE

Was the *New York Times* guilty of libel? After all, Sullivan was not named in the advertisement's criticism of police conduct. However, Sullivan argued that because he was the supervisor of the police department, criticism of the police was also directed at him. The Alabama jury had said the ad was unfair to Sullivan because it contained minor factual errors about the police actions.

THE DECISION

The Supreme Court rejected Sullivan's claim. It also established a new rule about when government officials can sue for libel. To win a libel suit, a public official must show that the defendant published its story with malice. In other words, either the defendant knew the story was false, or the defendant recklessly didn't bother to find out whether it was false.

defendant: *person against whom a charge is brought in a court*

THE IMPACT

The Supreme Court's decision expanded the freedom of the press. The press was now able to investigate government officials and report on important issues without constantly having to worry about lawsuits. The decision also put an end to some $300 million of libel suits brought by southern officials disputing press coverage of segregation. The Court's decision required the press to report responsibly and accurately, but it ensured that reporting about the government wouldn't be stopped by fear of lawsuits.

? Do you think the Supreme Court's ruling was fair to government officials? Give reasons to support your answer.

Quick Fact

Under the Alabama state law, the *New York Times* could have avoided the libel suit if it had published a retraction in response to Sullivan's demand. The paper refused because there was no reference to Sullivan in the ad.

The Expert Says...

" *New York Times v. Sullivan* broadened the meaning of free speech and freedom of the press, giving Americans more room to think what they wish and say what they think than any other people. "

— Anthony Lewis, former *New York Times* columnist and two-time Pulitzer Prize winner

FREEDOM OF THE PRESS

U.S. POSTAGE 4¢

A Freedom of the Press commemorative stamp, 1958

10   9   8   7   6

STRONG PRESS AND FREE SPEECH

The following report discusses the reasoning behind the Supreme Court's ruling in New York Times v. Sullivan.

Justice Brennan of the Supreme Court wrote the opinion. He looked back to early American history to understand the meaning of freedom of the press. He found that many Founding Fathers had believed that citizens' basic freedoms depended on a strong press and free speech. Without these rights, the people could not debate current events and the government might act secretly. These rights were so important that the Founders adopted the First Amendment to the Constitution to protect them. That amendment stops Congress from limiting freedom of speech and freedom of the press.

Sullivan's lawsuit especially troubled the Court because he was a government official. Justice Brennan said that the First Amendment's most important role is allowing citizens to discuss and criticize their government. That's why the government is rarely allowed to censor the press, and cannot shut down publications it doesn't like. The Court worried that Sullivan's lawsuit was really an attempt to punish the *Times* for its reporting. Sullivan hadn't even been named by the paper, and the Court didn't believe that he had suffered any damage.

The Court threw out Sullivan's lawsuit and his $500,000 award. But it didn't totally ban government officials from filing libel suits. Instead, it made it much harder for them to win such cases. Because officials put themselves in the public eye, they have to accept that their actions will be debated and criticized. They can only sue for libel, therefore, when the press reports with malice — either by publishing statements that it knows are false, or that it hasn't bothered to verify.

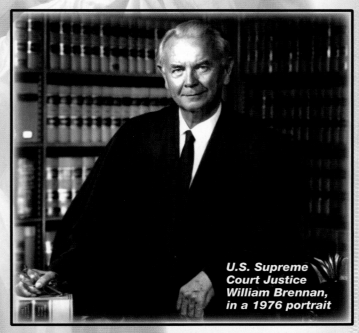

U.S. Supreme Court Justice William Brennan, in a 1976 portrait

? The Constitution says Congress can't limit free speech. In this case, the Supreme Court protected this right by making it very difficult for public officials to sue the press. But it didn't make it impossible. Why do you think the Court allowed some limits on the press?

Take Note

This case made headlines and takes the #3 spot. The landmark ruling in this case broadened freedom of the press, one of the most important rights of the American people. Without this important ruling, the press might have been too afraid of being sued to cover sensitive issues or public figures. As a result of the Court's decision, the press better understood both its freedom to report the news and its responsibility to do so without malice.

• Do you agree that this case is more significant than the 1974 Supreme Court ruling that led to the resignation of President Richard Nixon? Explain, using your own words.

5   4   **3**   2   1

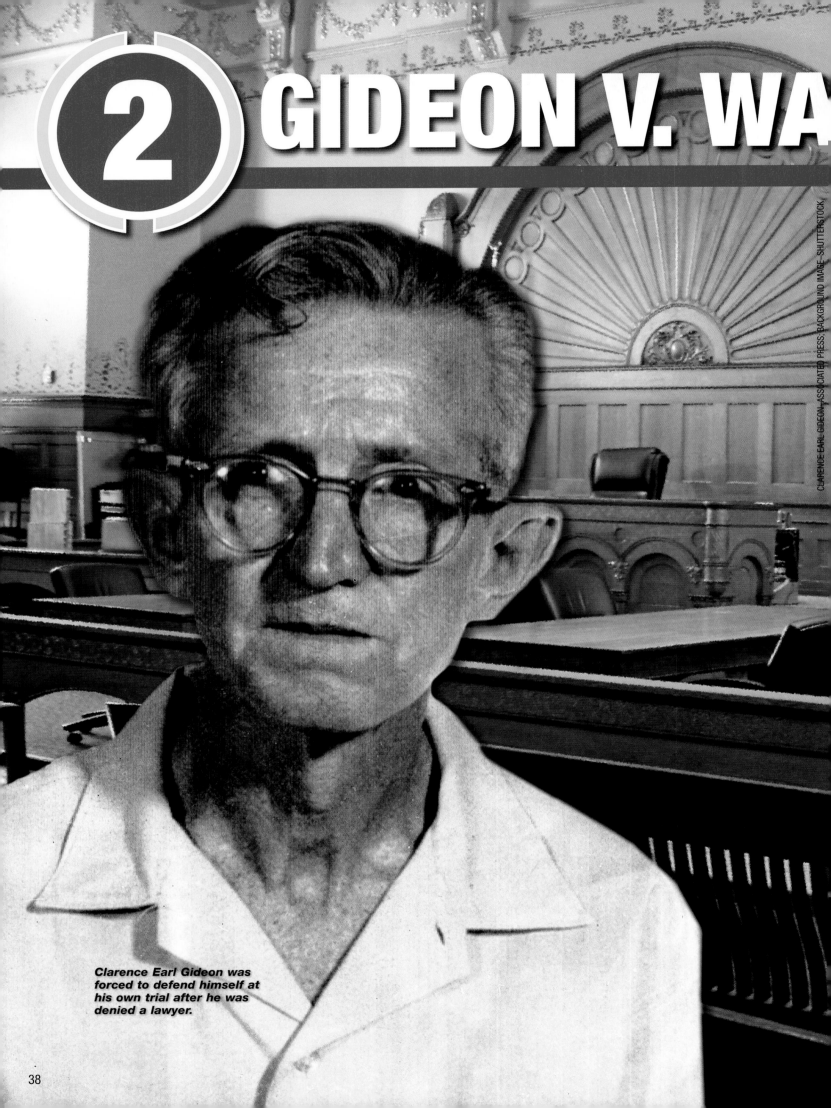

Clarence Earl Gideon was forced to defend himself at his own trial after he was denied a lawyer.

CLARENCE EARL GIDEON—ASSOCIATED PRESS; BACKGROUND IMAGE—SHUTTERSTOCK.

NWRIGHT

MOMENT OF TRUTH: On March 18, 1963, the Supreme Court of the United States granted Clarence Gideon's request to have a lawyer appointed to represent him in court.

WHAT'S MEMORABLE: The Court's ruling changed the public defender system and brought about a legal system that guarantees all criminal defendants a lawyer.

Do you ever watch courtroom dramas? Can you follow the arguments of the lawyers or understand their legal jargon?

Now, imagine finding yourself in a real courtroom, not as a spectator, but as a criminal defendant like Clarence Gideon. The prosecutor points an accusing finger at you. The black-robed judge peers down at you from behind his imposing desk. Expressionless jurors listen to arguments with your fate in their hands. This can be a strange and intimidating place, and your lawyer's role is to guide you through it. But for many years criminal defendants in state courts did not have a right to counsel. If they couldn't afford a lawyer, they were on their own.

In June 1961, Gideon was charged with robbing a pool hall in Panama City, Florida. The Florida court refused to grant him legal counsel, and he was too poor to hire his own lawyer. He had to defend himself in court.

Could a defendant have a fair trial without having proper legal advice? After Gideon was given the maximum five-year jail sentence, he took his case to the Supreme Court of the United States. "The question is very simple," he wrote. "I requested the court to appoint me [an] attorney and the court refused." He argued that this had denied him a fair trial.

---

jargon: *technical language specific to a particular profession, trade, or group*
counsel: *be represented by a lawyer when a person is on trial*

GIDEON V. WAINWRIGHT

THE ISSUE

The question was whether the U.S. Constitution requires a lawyer to be appointed for criminal defendants who can't afford one. This issue wasn't new to the U.S. Supreme Court. For many years, it had made decisions about which defendants had to be given a lawyer on a case-by-case basis.

THE DECISION

In *Gideon*, the Supreme Court finally stopped trying to decide which criminal defendants needed counsel and which didn't. It decided that the Sixth Amendment to the U.S. Constitution, which guarantees criminal defendants a fair trial, applied in all U.S. courts, both state and federal. It ruled that a trial's fairness depended, in part, on the accused being represented by an attorney. The decision was unanimous, and Gideon was granted a new trial.

THE IMPACT

The ruling led the states to develop public defender systems. These systems vary widely from state to state, but all are designed to give defendants as fair a trial as possible. Several other countries also adopted this practice. It was a major victory for all Americans and an important milestone in the history of the U.S. legal system. Gideon himself was tried again for the robbery. This time, he had a lawyer and was acquitted as there was little evidence against him.

acquitted: *found not guilty*

Quick Fact

Gideon had a lawyer at the Supreme Court. Abe Fortas was appointed to argue Gideon's case. He and his law firm worked on the case for months without charging legal fees. In 1965, Fortas became a Supreme Court justice.

? Abe Fortas knew he wouldn't be paid to represent Gideon, but he was eager to do so. Why might he have wanted to argue the case before the Supreme Court?

The Expert Says...

"If an obscure Florida convict named Clarence Earl Gideon had not sat down in his prison cell … to write a letter to the Supreme Court … the vast machinery of American law would have gone on functioning undisturbed. But Gideon did write that letter, the Court did look into his case … and the whole course of American legal history has been changed."

— Robert F. Kennedy, U.S. Attorney General, 1961–1964

? Gideon argued that he couldn't have a fair trial without a lawyer. But some people disagreed and thought juries might sympathize with defendants who had to represent themselves. What do you think?

Gideon wrote this petition asking the Chief Justice of the Supreme Court to hear his case.

GIDEON'S TRUMPET

CLARENCE GIDEON WAS A DRIFTER IN SOCIETY — BUT HE WAS RESPONSIBLE FOR ONE OF THE LANDMARK CASES IN U.S. LEGAL HISTORY. HERE IS A PROFILE OF THE MAN.

DRIFTING

Gideon was born in Missouri on August 30, 1910. He ran away from home when he was a teenager. He was involved in petty crimes and was in and out of jail.

SETTLING DOWN

Gideon married four times. In the mid-1950s, he settled in Texas, where he was employed as tugboat laborer and bartender. Then he moved to Florida, where he became an electrician.

FACING TRIAL

In June 1961, Gideon was charged with robbing a pool hall. He had to defend himself because he was too poor to pay for counsel. He was sentenced to five years in jail by trial judge Robert McCrary Jr. During his prison term, Gideon studied the U.S. legal system and became convinced that he had a constitutional right to counsel. Gideon wrote to the Supreme Court of the United States asking it to review his case. In 1963, the Court ruled in his favor.

AFTER THE SUPREME COURT

In the end, Gideon was acquitted of the pool hall robbery. He died in 1972, at age 61. In 1964 Anthony Lewis wrote a book entitled *Gideon's Trumpet* about the *Gideon v. Wainwright* case. It won an Edgar Award for best fact-crime book, and was made into a television movie.

Quick Fact

At the time of Gideon's trial, many other U.S. states had already provided criminal defendants with legal counsel. In fact, the top law enforcers for 23 states wrote in support of Gideon's position.

Take Note

The *Gideon* case makes its way to the #2 spot. It clarified some of the constitutional rights of criminal defendants, such as the right to counsel, due process, and a fair trial. The Supreme Court's ruling made access to legal counsel a fundamental right in the United States. The ruling led to public defender systems that were adopted by many countries in the world.
• What advantages and disadvantages might people without legal training have if asked to defend themselves in court?

5   4   3   **2**   1

1 BROWN V. BOARD

Sisters Linda and Terry Lynn Brown sitting outside Monroe Elementary, their racially segregated school in Topeka, Kansas

LINDA & TERRY LYNN BROWN AT SCHOOL—CARL IWASAKI/TIME & LIFE PICTURES/GETTY IMAGES

OF EDUCATION OF TOPEKA

NEWSFLASH: SIX-YEAR-OLD IN A SUIT AGAINST SEGREGATION

MOMENT OF TRUTH: Tired of case-by-case decisions, the Supreme Court of the United States issued its decision on May 17, 1954.

WHAT'S MEMORABLE: The ruling's influence went beyond education. It paved the way for the Civil Rights Movement, which had an impact on all aspects of American life.

Physically segregating people by skin color was once a common practice in American society. For example, African-American and white students were separated and could not attend the same public schools. African Americans had to attend schools for African-American students, even if a school for white students was closer to their homes. Schools for African-American children had fewer resources and inferior facilities compared to schools for white students.

Linda Brown of Topeka, Kansas, was a case in point. Seven blocks from her house stood a school for the neighborhood's white children. But because she was black, she wasn't allowed to enroll there. Instead, the six-year-old Brown had to walk three times that distance every day, just to get to the bus that took her to her black elementary school.

Linda Brown's father joined other African-American parents in filing a class action lawsuit against the Board of Education of Topeka. The district court heard the case on June 25 and 26, 1951. It ruled in favor of the Board of Education. The parents then appealed that decision to the Supreme Court of the United States. It made a ruling whose influence would reach far beyond the segregation of public schools. Read on to find out how this case earns the #1 ranking on our list.

class action: *a lawsuit brought by one or more people on behalf of themselves and everyone else who shares the identical interest*

BROWN V. BOARD OF EDUCATION OF TOPEKA

THE ISSUE

The Supreme Court had to determine whether racial segregation, which required that white and African-American students attend separate schools, violated the Equal Protection Clause of the 14th Amendment to the Constitution. According to the 14th Amendment, "No state shall … deny to any person within its jurisdiction the equal protection of the laws."

THE DECISION

The Supreme Court ruled that the opportunity of public education "must be made available to all on equal terms." It also struck down the Board of Education's argument that separate schools for African Americans prepared them for the segregation they would face during their adult lives.

jurisdiction: *territory within which authority is exercised*

? The Board of Education argued that segregation was a fact of life, so its black students might as well get used to it as early as possible. Do you think it's ever okay to accept an injustice instead of working to fix it? Explain.

Quick Fact

The NAACP (National Association for the Advancement of Colored People) recruited Brown and other African-American parents for the class-action suit against the Board of Education of Topeka. Thurgood Marshall was the NAACP's Chief Counsel and he argued the case before the Supreme Court. In 1967, Marshall was appointed a justice of the Supreme Court of the United States.

The Expert Says...

" *Brown v. Board of Education* was a thunderbolt, a decision with as powerful an impact on society as any judgment of the Supreme Court — or very likely any court — had ever issued. "

— Anthony Lewis, author of *Make No Law*

Linda Brown Smith, at age nine

THE IMPACT

The Supreme Court's ruling did not result in immediate desegregation of America's public schools. In fact, the decision met with massive resistance. In 1963, Alabama Governor George Wallace personally blocked the main door to Foster Auditorium at the University of Alabama to prevent the enrollment of two African-American students. But the ruling ultimately ended segregation in public schools, and led to the full desegregation of Americans' daily life. *Brown v. Board of Education of Topeka* was a giant step forward in the American Civil Rights Movement.

? If you had been reporting the *Brown* case for a newspaper on May 17, 1954, what headline would you have chosen?

Quick Fact

Because schools were segregated across the country, Topeka's weren't the only ones attacked in the courts. The Supreme Court actually joined four other cases to the Browns' — dealing with schools in Delaware, South Carolina, Virginia, and Washington, D.C. — and decided all five cases together.

Does Separate Mean Unequal?

Although *Brown v. Board of Education of Topeka* marked a major victory for African Americans, integration of the schools took time. Fourteen years after the ruling, only 20 percent of African-American students in the South attended integrated schools. By the 1980s, most Americans finally fully accepted the Supreme Court's ruling as the correct decision. Today, it is hailed as one of the greatest and most important decisions in the history of the Supreme Court. These fact cards describe its impact.

Ending Segregation

The ruling struck down the "separate but equal" doctrine, which allowed a state to segregate whites and blacks by providing separate but equal facilities for African Americans. Chief Justice Earl Warren argued that segregation clearly gave African-American children "a feeling of inferiority as to their status in the community that may affect their hearts and minds in a way unlikely to ever be undone," even if segregated schools gave them access to equal physical facilities. Warren reasoned that separate facilities, in and of themselves, deprived students of equal educational opportunities.

Quick Fact

In *Brown*, the Supreme Court decided that segregated schools were illegal, but it didn't say how to fix these schools. Instead, it let local school boards figure out how to desegregate their schools. It also ordered local courts to police these efforts. Unfortunately, this led to years of lawsuits about school desegregation, and, in many areas, little progress was made.

Inspiring Civil Rights

The Supreme Court's decision met massive and sometimes violent resistance in the South. For example, Prince Edward County, Virginia, closed all of its public schools — white and black — rather than integrate. This resistance, however, showed many people the real ugliness of segregation and fueled the growth of the Civil Rights Movement. This resulted in educational and business opportunities and a growing middle class of African Americans and other groups.

Promoting Human Rights

For 60 years, the "separate but equal" doctrine separated whites and African Americans in education, housing, transportation, business, and employment. The Supreme Court's decision made this form of discrimination illegal. It raised the country's image abroad and inspired human rights struggles around the world.

Take Note

Brown v. Board of Education of Topeka takes the #1 spot on our list. The Supreme Court ruled against public school segregation. The laws, policies, and practices struck down by this Court had far-reaching implications. The ruling began to change attitudes and beliefs in the United States, inspired the Civil Rights Movement, and promoted human rights struggles around the world.

- Compare *Brown v. Board of Education of Topeka* with another case in the book. Do you think *Brown* should take the #1 ranking? What factors did you consider?

5   4   3   2   1

We Thought …

Here are the criteria we used in ranking the 10 most memorable court cases in U.S. history.

The court case:
• Played a crucial role in the development of a new law
• Affected the rights of individuals in American society
• Brought about a change in American society
• Influenced other cases that came after
• Captured the interest of the media
• Involved interesting facts and information
• Is studied by law students

New York Times v. Sul
Montgomery's Police Chief

What Do You Think?

1. Do you agree with our ranking? If you don't, try ranking the court cases yourself. Justify your ranking with data from your own research and reasoning. You may refer to our criteria, or you may want to draw up your own list of criteria.

2. Here are three other court cases we considered but in the end did not include in our top 10 list: *Scopes v. Tennessee*, *Regents of the University of California v. Bakke*, and *New York Times v. United States*.
   - Find out more about them. Do you think these cases should have made our list? Give reasons for your response.
   - Are there other court cases you think should have made our list? Explain your choices.

Index

A

African Americans, 35, 43–45
Aggravated damages, 16
Aiuto, Russell, 28
Alabama, 35–36, 44
Albuquerque, 15–17
Alibi, 27

B

Bailiff, 5
Bernstein, Carl, 31–32
Betamax Case, 22–25
Board of Education of Topeka, 42–45
Brennan, William, 37
Brown, Linda, 42–45

C

Chief Justice, 28–29, 40, 45
Civil rights, 35, 43–45
Commonwealth, 26–29
Compensation, 10, 12–13, 16–17
Congress, 20, 30, 32–33, 36–37
Contempt of court, 31
Copyright, 23–25
Counsel, 39–41, 44
Court of Appeals, 11–12, 21, 24
Court order, 31

D

Damage, 12, 16, 25, 35, 37
Defendant, 16, 28, 36, 39–41
Defense, 16, 21, 29
Discrimination, 35, 45
Dispute, 5, 31, 33
Due process, 28, 41
Dukakis, Governor Michael, 28

E

Endangered Species Act (ESA), 18–21
England, 28
Environmental, 19–21
Evidence, 5, 27–28, 31–32, 40

F

Fair use, 24–25
First Amendment, 35, 37
Flood, Curt, 6–9
Florida, 39–41
Ford, President Gerald, 30
Fortas, Abe, 40
Fourteenth Amendment, 44
Free agency system, 7–9
Free speech, 36–37

G

Gideon, Clarence Earl, 38–41
Gideon's Trumpet, 41
Guilty, 5, 27–29, 33, 36, 40

H

Haldeman, H. D., 33
Hill, Hank, 18–21

I

Infringement, 23–25
Injury, 10, 12, 16
Innocent, 5

J

Jail, 26, 39, 41
Jaworski, Leon, 32
Judge, 5, 12, 16, 27–28, 31–32, 39, 41
Judgment, 15, 19, 27, 35, 44
Jury, 5, 12, 15–17, 27–28, 36

K

Kansas, 42–43
Kennedy, Robert F., 40
Kuhn, Bowie K., 6–9

L

Lawsuit, 11, 16–17, 23–24, 35–37, 43, 45
Leonard, Andrew, 20
Lewis, Anthony, 36, 41, 44
Libel, 34–37
Liebeck, Stella, 14–17
Little Tennessee River, 18–21
Long Island Railroad Company, 10–13

M

MacKenzie, John P., 32
Magna Carta, 32
Major League Baseball, 6–9
Malice, 36–37
Marshall, Thurgood, 44
Massachusetts, 28
McDonald's Corporation, 14–17
Media, 5, 16, 23, 46

N

Native Cherokee Nation, 19
Negligence, 11–13, 16
New York, 11–12
New York Times, 34–37, 47
Nixon, President Richard, 30–33, 37

P

Palsgraf, Barbara, 13
Palsgraf, Helen, 10–13
Palsgraf, William Jr., 13
Palsgraf, William III, 13
Petition, 19, 40
Pfeifer, Paul E., 12
Precedent, 8
Press, 5, 35–37
Prison, 5, 29, 40–41
Prosecutor, 31–32, 39
Pulitzer Prize, 32, 36

R

Reserve clause, 7–9

S

Sacco, Nicola, 26–29
Segregation, 35–36, 43–45
Sixth Amendment, 40
Snail darter, 18–21
Sony Corporation, 22–25
Stella Award, 14–17
St. Louis, 7
Sullivan, L. B., 34–37

T

Tellico Dam, 18–21
Tennessee, 18–21
Tennessee Valley Authority (TVA), 18–21
Thayer, Webster, 27–29
Thorn, John, 8
Tort, 12–13, 16

U

Universal City Studios, Inc., 22–25

V

Vanzetti, Bartolomeo, 26–29
Verdict, 12, 15, 27–29
Von Lohmann, Fred, 24

W

Wallace, Governor George, 44
Warren, Earl, 28, 45
Washington, 9, 29, 31, 44
Washington Post, 32
Watergate, 30–33
White House, 31–33
Woodward, Bob, 31–32